najc

NEPTUNE

Far, Far Away

by Joyce Markovics

Consultant: Karly M. Pitman, PhD
Planetary Science Institute
Tucson, Arizona

PUBLISHING

New York, New York

Credits

Cover, © NASA/JPL; TOC, © NASA/JPL; 5, © NASA; 6–7, © Wikipedia & Nasa; 8, © NASA/SDO (AIA); 9, © NASA/JPL; 11, © NASA/Voyager 2 Team; 12–13, © NASA; 14, © NASA/JPL; 15, © NASA/JPL; 16–17, © NASA/JPL/U.S. Geological Survey, Voyager 2, NASA; 18, © NASA/JPL; 20–21, © NASA/JPL; 23TL, © Kritchanut/Shutterstock; 23TM, © Ivan Tykhyi/Thinkstock; 23BL, © NASA/JPL; 23BR, © iStock/Thinkstock.

Publisher: Kenn Goin
Senior Editor: Joyce Tavolacci
Creative Director: Spencer Brinker
Design: Deborah Kaiser
Photo Researcher: Michael Win

Library of Congress Cataloging-in-Publication Data

Markovics, Joyce L., author.
  Neptune : far, far away / by Joyce Markovics.
     pages cm. — (Out of this world)
  Includes bibliographical references and index.
  ISBN 978-1-62724-568-5 (library binding) — ISBN 1-62724-568-5 (library binding)
  1. Neptune (Planet)—Juvenile literature. I. Title.
  QB691.M37 2015
  523.48—dc23
                                        2014037727

For more information, write to Bearport Publishing Company, Inc., 45 West 21st Street, Suite 3B, New York, New York 10010. Printed in the United States of America.

10 9 8 7 6 5 4 3 2 1

CONTENTS

What planet is farthest
from Earth?

NEPTUNE!

Neptune is part of Earth's Solar System.

JUPITER

MARS

VENUS

EARTH

MERCURY

SUN

6

SATURN

NEPTUNE

URANUS

It's the eighth planet
from the Sun.

Neptune is very cold,
partly because it's so
far from the Sun.

sun

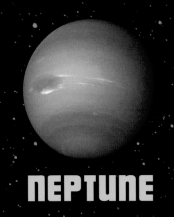

NEPTUNE

The temperature can dip below –361°F (–218°C).

Neptune is the windiest planet in the Solar System.

Winds whip around at more than 1,297 miles per hour (2,087 kph)!

Windstorms

Fifty-seven Earths could fit inside Neptune.

EARTH

That's one big planet!

NEPTUNE

13

Six rings circle Neptune.

Rings

Two of Neptune's rings

The rings are made of ice, dust, and other bits of matter.

Neptune has many moons.

Scientists have counted up to 14 so far.

There may be even more.

Two of Neptune's moons

People cannot live on Neptune.

WHY?

It's covered with blue clouds made from poisonous gases.

Only one spacecraft, Voyager 2, has visited Neptune.

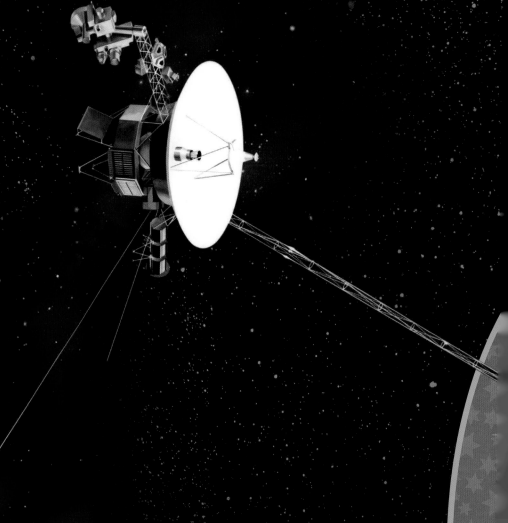

A photo of Neptune taken by *Voyager 2*

It took 12 years for it to reach the big, blue planet.

That's because Neptune is so far away!

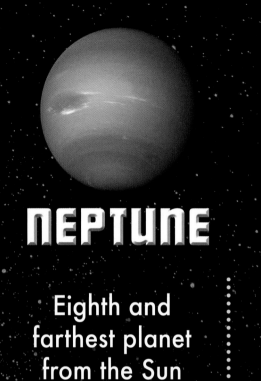

NEPTUNE  EARTH

NEPTUNE	VERSUS	EARTH
Eighth and farthest planet from the Sun	POSITION	Third planet from the Sun
30,599 miles (49,244 km) across	SIZE	7,918 miles (12,743 km) across
About -328°F (-200°C)	AVERAGE TEMPERATURE	59°F (15°C)
Fourteen—and possibly more!	NUMBER OF MOONS	One

GLOSSARY

matter (MAT-ur) anything that has weight and takes up space; what things are made of

poisonous (POI-zuhn-uhss) able to kill or harm a living thing

Solar System (SOH-lur SISS-tuhm) the Sun and everything that circles around it, including the eight planets

spacecraft (SPAYSS-kraft) a vehicle that can travel in space

temperature (TEM-pur-uh-chur) how hot or cold something is

INDEX

READ MORE

Chrismer, Melanie.
Neptune (Scholastic News Nonfiction Readers). New York: Children's Press (2008).

Lawrence, Ellen.
Neptune: The Stormiest Planet (Zoom Into Space). New York: Ruby Tuesday Books (2014).

LEARN MORE ONLINE

To learn more about Neptune, visit
www.bearportpublishing.com/OutOfThisWorld

ABOUT THE AUTHOR

Joyce Markovics has written more than 30 books for young readers. She lives along the Hudson River in Tarrytown, New York.